Simple Easy Paleo

Fast Fabulous Paleo Recipes with 5 Ingredients or Less

By Sasha Kendrick

Disclaimer

The recipes within this book are for information purposes only and are not meant as a diet to treat, prescribe or diagnose illness. Please seek the advice of a doctor or alternative health care professional if you have any health issues you would like addressed.

Table of Contents

Introduction

Thank you for purchasing *Simple Easy Paleo: Fast Fabulous Paleo Recipes with 5 Ingredients or Less.*

I don't know about you, but I start to lose interest in cooking when I see a long list of ingredients, or if many of them are hard to find. Taking the time to make a grocery list that runs a mile long just isn't going to happen for most us.

The problem is that complicated recipes can get in the way of us eating healthily as, put off by this complicated process of cooking, we reach for the nearest packaged food. Not so with the recipes in this book!

Inside here, you will find twenty-five delicious recipes that are extremely simple and easy to make, because they only contain five ingredients (or less). No more going back and forth to the fridge or the pantry. No more searching online for some strange ingredient you'll only use once. Whoever said that eating healthy was hard or complicated, needs a copy of this book!

There are starters, entrées, side dishes, desserts and treats all made with five or fewer ingredients so you can rustle up a three-course meal in no time at all.

If you are new to the Paleo diet, this book will help you learn to eat like our caveman (or woman) ancestors so that your body is supported by optimal nutrition and great health by including only foods that could be hunted or gathered from the natural environment.

Read on to discover a collection of delicious recipes with all-natural ingredients, that will allow your genes to express themselves optimally, giving you health and energy to spare. Get ready to bring a burst of nutrition, flavor and convenience into your daily life. Enjoy!

What is the Paleo Diet?

The Paleo diet operates from the premise that we have moved away from a diet that supports optimal functioning of our bodies.

This has lead to an explosion in rates of disease, obesity and a reliance on substances like sugar and caffeine to help us meet the demands of a 21st century lifestyle.

Advocates of the diet claim that we can bring our bodies back into balance, keep it well-nourished and disease-free by eating a diet that resembles that of our hunter-gatherer ancestors.

The Paleo diet is a modern interpretation of that diet using real food ingredients and avoidance of processed, chemical-laden foods.

Foods to eat:

Meat

Fish

Fowl

Eggs

Vegetables

Fruits

Nuts

Seeds

Healthy fats

Foods to avoid:

Grains

Sugar

Legumes

Dairy

Processed food

Alcohol

Starches

Vegetable oils

What you eat, and, for some who take the basic principle further, how much you sleep, work, relax and play, all fall under the Paleo banner.

We are learning more and more about how our current lifestyle makes us fat, sick, weak and miserable; and how important it is to make a radical change.

Starters

Cajun Carrot Fries

Serves 8
Time involved: 10 minutes prepping; 30 minutes baking
Equipment needed: large bowl; baking sheet

Pre-heat the oven to 450°F.

Ingredients

8 large carrots (peeled and sliced into thin pieces, like "fries")
1 tablespoon olive oil
1/4 teaspoon cayenne pepper (optional)
Salt (to taste)
Black pepper (to taste)

Directions

In a large bowl; add and toss the sliced carrots, olive oil, cayenne pepper (optional), salt and black pepper (to taste).

Next, arrange the fries on your baking sheet in a single layer.

Bake for about 15 minutes, flip over and bake again for another 10 to 15 minutes until crisp.

Nutrition Facts
Calories: 44, Fat: 1.9g, Carbs: 6.9g, Protein: 0.7g

Bacon Avocado Bites

Serves 5
Time involved: 15 minutes prepping; 8 minutes baking
Equipment needed: large bowl; baking sheet

Pre-heat the oven to 425°F.

Ingredients

1 avocado
10 bacon strips (cooked but not crispy)

Directions

Remove the skin of the avocado and slice the flesh in half. Cut each half into 5 strips.

Wrap each strip in a piece of bacon carefully. Tuck the end piece in place.

Bake for about 8 minutes.

Nutrition Facts
Calories: 78, Fat: .6.6g, Carbs: 3.2g, Protein: 2.4g

Serves 15
Time involved: 10 minutes prepping; 20 minutes cooking
Equipment needed: large pan; sharp knife

Ingredients

2 pounds chestnuts
Coconut oil (as needed)
1/4 cup water
Salt (to taste)

Directions

First, using a sharp knife cut an "X" into one side of each chestnut to permit the steam caused by roasting to escape.

Toss the chestnuts with the coconut oil.

Heat a large pan over low heat until hot. Add in the chestnuts, cover and cook for about 15 minutes; stir frequently.

Now add in the water and cover, continue to roast for about 5 minutes until the water is evaporated and chestnuts are tender.

Finally, serve the chestnuts hot and sprinkled with salt.

Nutrition Facts
Calories: 126, Fat: 1.7g, Carbs: 26.7g, Protein: 1.0g

Paleo Shrimp Cocktail

Serves 8
Time involved: 10 minutes prepping; 5 minutes cooking
Equipment needed: large pan

Ingredients

2 pounds large shrimp (cleaned, peeled, de-veined with tail on)
2 cups puréed tomatoes
2 tablespoons mustard (Dijon)
1 tablespoon horseradish
2 teaspoons lemon juice

Directions

In large pan, add water and bring to a boil.

Add in the shrimp and cook for about 3 to 5 minutes or until the shrimp turns pink and curls slightly; stir occasionally.

Drain, let it cool.

Combine the puréed tomatoes, horseradish, mustard and lemon juice and mix well.

Serve shrimp with sauce on the side.

Nutrition Facts
Calories: 140, Fat: 2g, Carbs: 5g, Protein: 25g

Paleo Mushroom Crunchies

Serves 6
Time involved: 15 minutes prepping; 45 minutes baking
Equipment needed: 2 baking sheets; 2 parchment papers; brush; knife

Pre-heat the oven to 300°F.

Ingredients

3 3/4 cups mushrooms
6 tablespoons ghee/oil (melted)
Kosher salt (to taste)
Freshly ground pepper (to taste)

Directions

Line the baking sheets with parchment paper. Slice the mushrooms in half laterally into 1/8" inch slices.

Arrange the slices on the parchment-lined baking sheets in a single layer, about 1 inch apart.

Brush the melted ghee/oil on both sides of the mushroom slices and season with salt and pepper (to taste).

Bake in the oven for about 45 minutes, until nicely golden and crispy.

Nutrition Facts
Calories: 48, Fat: 4.4g, Carbs: 1.6g, Protein: 1.6g

Entrées

Chicken and Kale Soup

Serves 6
Time involved: 10 minutes prepping; 7 hours cooking
Equipment needed: knife, cutting board, slow cooker

Ingredients

2 pounds chicken thigh meat
2 sweet potatoes (cut into chunks)
1 onion (diced)
1 tablespoon tomato paste
3 cups kale

Directions

Add the chicken pieces to the slow cooker.

Chop the onion and potato chunks and add those in.

Add the tomato paste and mix it in.

Cook for 6 hours on low.

Stir everything, shred the chicken, and mix in the kale.

Cook 45 minutes longer, then enjoy.

Nutrition Facts
Calories: 272, Fat: 6g, Carbs: 23g, Protein: 32g

Serves 6
Time involved: 10 minutes prepping; 25 minutes cooking
Equipment needed: skillet

Ingredients

12 sausage links
1 yellow bell pepper
3 garlic cloves (minced)
2 teaspoon oregano (dried)
2 teaspoon thyme (dried)

Directions

In a skillet; add and sauté the sausage over medium heat. Once the sausage is cooked, drain any grease from the pan.

Slice the yellow pepper into pieces and add them into the skillet with the sausages.

Sprinkle the dried oregano and thyme into the skillet; cover and sauté on low for 5 to 8 minutes.

Finally, add in the minced garlic and cook for another 3 to 5 minutes.

Nutrition Facts
Calories: 117, Fat: 0.1g, Carbs: 4.3g, Protein: 4.4g

Serves 6
Time involved: 10 minutes prepping; 30 minutes cooking + baking
Equipment needed: skillet; spoon; casserole dish or muffin tins; foil

Pre-heat the oven up to 350°F.

Ingredients

6 tomatoes
1 pound ground sausage
5 button mushrooms (diced)
1 medium yellow onion (diced)
2 garlic cloves (minced)

Directions

In a skillet; add and brown the onions over medium heat.

Add in the sausage and brown.

Stir in the mushrooms, and sauté until softened.

Next, remove the tops of each tomato and scoop out half of the core. Place the scooped out parts into the skillet.

Add in the garlic once the sausage is fully browned, and continue cooking until the garlic is fragrant.

Now, spoon the sausage mixture into the tomatoes, and place them in a casserole dish or in muffin tins.

Finally, cover the dish with foil and bake for about 15 minutes.

Nutrition Facts
Calories: 291, Fat: 21.7g, Carbs: 7.3g, Protein: 16.4g

Baked Salmon Fillets Dijon

Serves 4
Time involved: 10 minutes prepping; 15 minutes baking
Equipment needed: shallow baking pan; aluminum foil

Pre-heat the oven to 400°F.

Ingredients

4 (4 ounce) fillets salmon
3 tablespoons Dijon mustard
Salt
Pepper to taste (to taste)
1/4 cup olive oil

Directions

First, line a shallow baking pan with aluminum foil. Place the salmon skin-side down on the foil.

Spread a thin layer of mustard on top of each fillet and season with salt and pepper (to taste). Then drizzle with oil.

Bake in the oven for about 15 minutes or until the salmon flakes easily with a fork.

Nutrition Facts
Calories: 331, Fat: 21.5g, Carbs: 7.5g, Protein: 25g

Chicken Salad

Serves 6
Time involved: 20 minutes prepping
Equipment needed: bowl

Ingredients

1 avocado (mashed)
2 cups chopped chicken (cooked)
1/2 cup celery (finely chopped)
1/4 cup red onion (finely chopped)
1 teaspoon lemon juice

Directions

In a bowl, add and combine the five ingredients together. Mix well.

This tastes great as the filling in a lettuce wrap or straight out of a bowl

Nutrition Facts
Calories: 136, Fat: 7.2g, Carbs: 3.3g, Protein: 13.8g

Side Dishes

Glazed Parsnips

Serves 6
Time involved: 5 minutes prepping; 25 minutes cooking
Equipment needed: large pot; skillet

Ingredients

1 pound parsnips (peeled)
1 tablespoon olive oil
4 tablespoons honey

Directions

Place the parsnips into a large pot, cover with water and bring to a boil.

Reduce the heat to medium-low and simmer for about 15 minutes or until tender. Drain, let it cool slightly, and then remove the parsnips and slice them into 2 ½ inches sticks.

Now, heat the oil in a skillet over medium heat. Stir in the honey and parsnips; toss well to coat.

Nutrition Facts
Calories: 143, Fat: 3.2g, Carbs: 28.1g, Protein: 1.9g

Serves 2
Time involved: 10 minutes prepping; 30 minutes cooking
Equipment needed: small pan; skillet; strainer

Ingredients

1 cup fresh green beans (topped and tailed)
1/4 cup bacon (chopped)
1 tablespoon almond butter

Directions

In a small pan, add water and bring it to a boil. Then, add in the green beans and boil them for about 5 minutes.

In the skillet; add the chopped bacon and cook until browned.

Drain the green beans in the strainer and add the almond butter into the skillet with the chopped bacon and stir to combine.

Lastly, stir in the green beans and mix well.

Nutrition Facts
Calories: 136, Fat: 9.6g, Carbs: 4.5g, Protein: 8.2g

Crispy Asparagus

Serves 4
Time involved: 15 minutes prepping; 25 minutes frying
Equipment needed: 2 shallow bowls; frying pan; tongs

Ingredients

16 asparagus spears
1 large egg
1/2 cup almond flour
Pepper to taste
Coconut oil for frying

Directions

Snap off the woody ends of the asparagus. Beat the egg and add into a shallow bowl.

Mix the almond flour and pepper in a second, shallow bowl.

Dip each asparagus spear into the egg and then into the flour.

Heat coconut oil in a frying pan over medium high heat.

Add each spear of asparagus into the oil and brown for about 2 minutes per side. Serve.

Nutrition Facts
Calories: 136, Fat: 12g, Carbs: 4g, Protein: 4.5g

Serves 6
Time involved: 15 minutes prepping; 25 minutes boiling
Equipment needed: large bowl; food processor; large pot

Ingredients

1 head of cauliflower
2 garlic cloves (minced)
Sea salt to taste
3 tablespoons olive oil

Directions

Bring a large pot of water to a boil.

Add the cauliflower and boil for about 15 minutes, until soft.

Transfer the cauliflower to the food processor and pulse until smooth.

Add garlic cloves, salt and olive oil and pulse until smooth.

Serve!

Nutrition Facts
Calories: 80, Fat: 7g, Carbs: 4g, Protein: 2g

Roasted Butternut Squash

Serves 4
Time involved: 15 minutes prepping; 25 minutes baking
Equipment needed: large bowl; baking sheet

Pre-heat the oven to 400°F.

Ingredients

1 butternut squash (peeled, seeded and sliced into 1-inch cubes)
2 tablespoons olive oil
2 garlic cloves (minced)
Salt (to taste)
Ground black pepper (to taste)

Directions

Toss the butternut squash with olive oil and garlic in a large bowl. Season it with salt and black pepper (to taste).

Arrange the coated squash onto a baking sheet.

Place into the oven and roast for about 25 minutes until the squash is tender and lightly browned.

Nutrition Facts
Calories: 177, Fat: 7g, Carbs: 30.3g, Protein: 2.6g

Dessert

Coconut Macaroons

Serves 10
Time involved: 20 minutes prepping; 1 hour refrigeration
Equipment needed: saucepan; baking sheet

Ingredients

1/2 cup coconut oil
1/2 cup coconut cream concentrate
1 cup shredded coconut (unsweetened)
1 tablespoon raw honey

Directions

Heat the oil and butter in a saucepan over medium heat so they soften.

Remove from the heat, and stir in the honey.

Slowly stir in the coconut until the consistency is desirable.

Line a baking sheet with parchment paper, shape the macaroons and line them up on the baking sheet.

Refrigerate to set.

Nutrition Facts
Calories: 183, Fat: 18g, Carbs: 5g, Protein: .9g

Tropical Pops

Serves 6
Time involved: 10 minutes prepping; 1 hour freezing
Equipment needed: blender; popsicle mold

Ingredients

1/2 pineapple (peeled and chopped)
1 14 oz. can coconut milk (full-fat)
1/2 banana
1/2 cup unsweetened shredded coconut
Raw honey

Directions

Combine all ingredients except the shredded coconut in a blender. Blend until it becomes smooth.

Stir in the shredded coconut.

Pour into popsicle molds and freeze for one hour.

Enjoy!

Nutrition Facts
Calories: 241, Fat: 22g, Carbs: 13g, Protein: 2.5g

Coconut Ice Cream with Walnuts and Dark Chocolate

Serves 8
Time involved: 10 minutes prepping; 30 minutes freezing
Equipment needed: small skillet; skillet; ice cream maker

Ingredients

2 cups pure coconut milk (chilled)
1/2 cup raw honey
1 cup walnuts (chopped)
1 cup coconut flakes (unsweetened)
2 tablespoons raw cocoa powder

Directions

Place the chopped walnuts into a small skillet and cook on medium-low heat for about 3 minutes or until lightly browned; stir frequently. Remove and set aside.

Stir together the coconut milk and honey in an ice cream maker. Freeze for about 20- 30 minutes, or according to ice cream maker instructions. If you don't have an ice cream maker, place in freezer and stir every 20 minutes until mostly frozen.

Add the toasted walnuts, coconut flakes and cocoa powder to the ice cream maker during the last 5 minutes of freezing or when mostly frozen if working it by hand.

Nutrition Facts
Calories: 332, Fat: 25.3g, Carbs: 28.9g, Protein: 3.7g

Flourless Minted Chocolate Paleo Cake

Serves 8
Time involved: 10 minutes prepping; 45 minutes baking
Equipment needed: 9-inch cake pan; nonstick skillet; stand mixer

Pre-heat the oven up to 350°F.

Ingredients

3/4 cup coconut oil
2 teaspoons peppermint oil
2 tablespoons raw cocoa powder
6 eggs
1/4 cup pure maple syrup

Directions

Grease a 9-inch cake pan with coconut oil. In a double boiler, melt the coconut oil and mix in the cocoa powder.

Remove the oil mixture from the heat and stir in the peppermint oil.

Next, in a standing mixer, beat the eggs and syrup on high for about 7 to 10 minutes or until light and fluffy.

Turn the mixer to low and slowly add in the melted chocolate/mint mixture until all the chocolate is incorporated.

Pour into greased cake pan and bake for about 45 minutes or until the top begins to look dull. Remove from oven and cool.

Nutrition Facts
Calories: 447, Fat: 32.9g, Carbs: 32.1g, Protein: 7.4g

Cherry Vanilla Ice Cream

Serves 8
Time involved: 10 minutes prepping; 1-2 hours chilling
Equipment needed: large bowl; ice cream maker

Ingredients

2 (14 ounce) cans coconut milk (full fat)
1 cup raw honey
1 ½ teaspoon vanilla extract
2 cups fresh cherries (pitted and diced)

Directions

In a large bowl; add and combine the coconut milk, honey and vanilla; stir them well.

Place into the freezer and chill for about 1 to 2 hours.

Transfer to an ice-cream maker and process according to manufacturer directions (or place in freezer and stir every twenty minutes until almost set). Add in the diced cherries to the mixture during the last 5 to 10 minutes of processing or when mostly frozen if working it by hand.

Nutrition Facts
Calories: 245, Fat: 11.8g, Carbs: 37.8g, Protein: 1.3g

Treats

Raw Chocolate Almond Brownies

Serves 12
Time involved: 10 minutes prepping; 2 hours chilling
Equipment needed: food processor; 8"×8" pan

Ingredients

1 1/2 cups raw almonds
1 cup dates
1/2 cup almond butter
1/4 cup cocoa powder
Shredded coconut (unsweetened)

Directions

Place the almonds into a food processor and process until finely blended. Add in the dates, almond butter and cocoa powder; process again until completely mixed.

Then, firmly press into an 8"×8" pan and sprinkle with shredded coconut. Refrigerate for 2 hours to set.

Slice into 12 squares and store into the refrigerator up to a week.

Nutrition Facts
Calories: 177, Fat: 11.6g, Carbs: 16.8g, Protein: 5.9g

Chocolate Paleo Cookies

Serves 10
Time involved: 10 minutes prepping; 10 minutes baking
Equipment needed: medium bowl; 2 sheets of baking paper; cookie cutter or knife; baking tray; baking paper

Pre-heat the oven to 325°F.

Ingredients

1 cup almond flour
1 tablespoon cocoa powder
1/2 teaspoon cinnamon
1 tablespoon honey
2/3 cup almond butter

Directions

In a bowl; add and combine all the ingredients; mix them well. Roll the dough between two sheets of baking paper to a thickness about 1/4".

With a cookie cutter, make the cookies (re-roll the dough as needed to use all of it.)

Line a baking tray with baking paper, and place cookies about 1 inch apart.

Bake for about 8 to 10 minutes, and let them cool before serving.

Nutrition Facts
Calories: 80, Fat: 6.1g, Carbs: 4.1g, Protein: 0.1g

Serves 8
Time involved: 15 minutes prepping; 25 minutes baking
Equipment needed: baking sheet

Preheat the oven to 375°F.

Ingredients

8 brown Turkish figs (washed, dried and tops cut off)
2 tablespoons of raw honey
1 tablespoon coconut oil
1/2 teaspoon on pure vanilla extract

Directions

Cut the figs into quarters and arrange them on a baking sheet.

Mix the oil, honey and vanilla together in a small bowl.

Drizzle the honey mixture over the figs.

Roast for 25 minutes.

Nutrition Facts
Calories: 54, Fat: 1.8, Carbs: 10g, Protein: .3g

Caramel Dip

Serves 4
Time involved: 1 hour prepping; 10 minute processing
Equipment needed: food processor; bowl

Ingredients

1/2 cup dates
1/2 cup coconut milk (full fat)
2 tablespoon pure maple syrup
1 tablespoon coconut oil
1/3 teaspoon of sea salt

Directions

Start by pouring the coconut milk into a bowl and adding the dates. Let them soak for an hour.

Combine the dates, coconut oil, syrup, salt and about half of the milk in a food processor and blend.

Add more coconut milk to get the desired consistency.

Enjoy. Great for dipping apples in!

Nutrition Facts
Calories: 175, Fat: 9.5g, Carbs: 24g, Protein: 1g

Serves 12
Time involved: 5 minutes prepping; 2 hours freezing
Equipment needed: medium bowl; small baking dish or container

Ingredients

1/2 cup almond butter
1/4 cup coconut oil (melted)
3 tablespoons + 1 teaspoon honey or maple syrup
1/4 teaspoon sea salt
1 teaspoon vanilla

Directions

In a mixing bowl; add all the ingredients together and mix until smooth.

Pour the mixture into a small baking dish or container.

Cover and freeze until firm; slice before serving.

Nutrition Facts
Calories: 125, Fat: 9.9g, Carbs: 7.2g, Protein: 2.4g

Conclusion

Can you believe it?

It is amazing that you can make such great recipes simply, easily, without complication. And if you want to make your life (and dinner) even easier, you can circle back around and keep making these as often as you would like.

Why go for the candy bar filled with processed ingredients and no nutrients, when you can quickly and easily make your own treats that taste even better and are healthy for you right at home? Not only are they delicious, they are also guilt-free, as you provide your body with the vitamins and nutrients that it needs.

From the shrimp cocktail to the butter fudge, we hope you have enjoyed the delicious creations that can be cooked up from five ingredients or less. We hope that they will grace your meal and snack times for years to come.

Best of luck to you with your health endeavors. We thank you for sharing this collection of our favorite, no muss-no fuss, Paleo recipes.

Other Books by Sasha Kendrick

25 Days of Paleo Christmas Cookies and Other Holiday Indulgences: Your 25-Day Step-By-Step Guide to Creating Guilt-Free, Gluten-Free Sweets and Treats with Recipes Your Friends Will Be Begging For

Paleo Bacon Cookbook: Lose Weight * Get Healthy * Eat Bacon

Paleo Cravings: Your Favorite Comfort Foods Made Paleo

Paleo Easter Cookbook: Fast and Easy Recipes for Busy Moms

Paleo Party Food Cookbook: Make Your Friends Love You With Delicious & Healthy Party Food!

Paleo Pizza Cookbook: Lose Weight and Get Healthy by Eating the Food You Love

Paleo Valentine's Day Cookbook: Quick, Easy Recipes That Will Melt Your Lover's Heart

Simple Easy Paleo: Fast Fabulous Paleo Recipes with 5 Ingredients or Less

* * *

Other Books in the Paleo Kitchen and Health Series

Coconut Health Made Simple: Coconut Oil Cures & Health Hacks to Lose Weight, Lower Cholesterol, Improve Your Memory, Hair, & Skin

Break Free From Emotional Eating: Stop Overeating and Start Losing Weight

* * *

Available on Kindle and in paperback.

Books by Green Hills Press

Movie and TV Books in the British Drama series

Call The Midwife!: Your Backstage Pass to the Era and the Making of the PBS TV Series

Doctor Who: 200 Facts on the Characters and Making of the BBC TV Series

Downton Abbey: Your Backstage Pass to the Era and Making of the TV Series

Mr Selfridge: Your Backstage Pass to the True Harry Selfridge Story and Making of the PBS TV Series

Pride & Prejudice: Your Backstage Pass to Jane Austen's Novel and The Making of the BBC TV Series, Starring Colin Firth

Sherlock Lives! 100+ Facts on Sherlock and the Smash Hit BBC TV Series

The Bletchley Park Enigma: 200+ Facts on the Story of Alan Turing That Inspired The Smash Hit Movie "The Imitation Game" Starring Benedict Cumberbatch

Books in the Royals and Celebrities series

KATE: Loyal Wife, Royal Mother, Queen-In-Waiting

HARRY: Popstar Prince

One Direction: Your Backstage Pass To The Boys, The Band, And The 1D Phenomenon

* * *

Don't delay! Check them out today!

Made in the USA
San Bernardino, CA
10 April 2018